D1397866

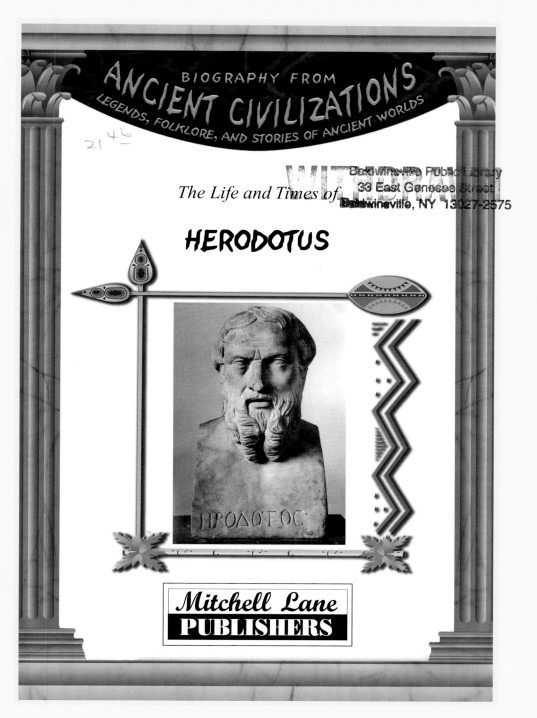

BIOGRAPHY FROM
ANCIENT CIVILIZATIONS
LEGENDS, FOLKLORE, AND STORIES OF ANCIENT WORLDS

The Life and Times of

HERODOTUS

ΠΡΟΔΟΤΟΣ

Mitchell Lane
PUBLISHERS

P.O. Box 196
Hockessin, Delaware 19707

Titles in the Series

The Life and Times of:

Alexander the Great	Herodotus
Archimedes	Hippocrates
Aristotle	Homer
Augustus Caesar	Joan of Arc
Buddha	Julius Caesar
Catherine the Great	King Arthur
Charlemagne	Marco Polo
Cicero	Moses
Cleopatra	Nero
Confucius	Pericles
Constantine	Plato
Genghis Khan	Rameses the Great
Hammurabi	Socrates

BIOGRAPHY FROM
ANCIENT CIVILIZATIONS
LEGENDS, FOLKLORE, AND STORIES OF ANCIENT WORLDS

The Life and Times of

HERODOTUS

Jim Whiting

Printing   1   2   3   4   5   6   7   8   9

Library of Congress Cataloging-in-Publication Data
Whiting, Jim, 1943–
    The life and time of Herodotus/by Jim Whiting.
       p.cm.—(Biography from ancient civilizations)
    Includes bibliographical references and index.
    ISBN 1-58415-509-4 (library bound: alk. paper)
1. Herodotus—Juvenile literature. 2. Historians—Greece—Biography—Juvenile literature. 3. Greece—History—Persian Wars, 500–449 B.C.—Juvenile literature. 4. History, Ancient—Juvenile literature. I. Title. II. Series.
D56.52.H45W45 2006
938.0072'02—dc22   DEC 11 2008
                                                                      2005036802
ISBN-10: 1-58415-509-4   ISBN-13: 978-1-58415-509-6

ABOUT THE AUTHOR: Jim Whiting has been a remarkably versatile and accomplished journalist, writer, editor, and photographer for more than 30 years. A voracious reader since early childhood, Mr. Whiting has written and edited about 200 nonfiction children's books. His subjects range from authors to zoologists and include contemporary pop icons and classical musicians, saints and scientists, emperors and explorers. Representative titles include *The Life and Times of Franz Liszt, The Life and Times of Julius Caesar, Charles Schulz*, and *Juan Ponce de Leon*.

    Other career highlights are a lengthy stint publishing *Northwest Runner*, the first piece of original fiction to appear in *Runners World* magazine, hundreds of descriptions and venue photographs for America Online, e-commerce product writing, sports editor for the *Bainbridge Island Review*, light verse in a number of magazines, and acting as the official photographer for the Antarctica Marathon.

    He lives in Washington state with his wife and two teenage sons.

PHOTO CREDITS: Cover, pp. 1, 3, 6—Getty Images; p. 9—Ellen Papakyriakou/ Anagnostou; p. 12—Andrea Pickens; pp. 15, 18—Getty Images; p. 21—Corbis; p. 26—Andrea Pickens; pp. 33, 38, 40—Corbis

PUBLISHER'S NOTE: This story is based on the author's extensive research, which he believes to be accurate. Documentation of such research is contained on page 46.

    The internet sites referenced herein were active as of the publication date. Due to the fleeting nature of some web sites, we cannot guarantee they will all be active when you are reading this book.

    To reflect current usage, we have chosen to use the secular era designations BCE ("before the common era") and CE ("of the common era") instead of the traditional designations BC ("before Christ") and AD (*anno Domini*, "in the year of the Lord").

The Life and Times of

HERODOTUS

Chapter 1	An Historic First and the First History	7
	FYInfo*: The Hoplites	11
Chapter 2	Sketching a Life	13
	FYInfo: The Ionion Greeks	17
Chapter 3	The World According to Herodotus	19
	FYInfo: The Dephic Oracle	25
Chapter 4	Jolting the Persian Juggernaut	27
	FYInfo: Triremes	37
Chapter 5	After Herodotus	39
	FYInfo: Thucydides and the Peloponnesian War	42
Chronology		43
Timeline in History		44
Chapter Notes		45
Further Reading		46
Glossary		47
Index		48

*For Your Information

Greek and Persian triremes clash during the Battle of Salamis in 480 BCE. Against all odds, the Greeks won a decisive victory. Herodotus spends a good portion of his famous book, "Histories," describing the battle and its significance.

CHAPTER
ONE

AN HISTORIC FIRST,
AND THE FIRST HISTORY

For hours the thousands of exhausted men trudged along the narrow dirt road. They had been up since dawn, and now it was midafternoon. The hot, late-summer sun beat down on them. There wasn't much water to quench their thirst. The first few miles of their trek had been flat, then the road began to rise. The uphill slog had continued for nearly ten miles.

Finally they reached the top of the long hill. The worst was over. Off in the distance they could see the outlines of their home city of Athens. The last few miles into the city sloped gently downhill. As they neared it, the jubilant inhabitants poured out with a heartfelt welcome. They clapped the men on the back and offered them brimming cups of cold water. Wives kissed their husbands, children waved to their fathers, parents warmly greeted their sons.

The men had no time to join the joyous celebration. They hadn't reached their final destination. They continued on for a few miles to the seashore and arrived just in time. Black specks appeared on the horizon. The specks transformed into hundreds of Persian galleys. Galleys were vessels propelled by dozens of oarsmen. Each boat contained fighting men bristling with weapons. The Athenians were also well armed. It was a standoff. The ships hovered just offshore. It is likely that the men shouted insults at one another.

Chapter ONE

It wasn't the first time the Athenians and Persians had faced each other on that September day in 490 BCE. When the sun rose, the two sides had been drawn up on a plain about twenty miles from Athens. The Athenians charged. It seemed a foolish thing to do. The Persians were the odds-on favorites to win: They had many more men than the Athenians. They were the ancient world's primary superpower. They felt confident that they would easily add Athens to their steadily growing empire.

The Athenians defied the odds. They employed superior tactics. Their soldiers, known as hoplites, broke the Persian lines. They killed thousands of their suddenly panic-stricken enemies. Fewer than 200 of their own men perished. The desperate Persian survivors clambered aboard their galleys and continued fighting. They knew they could still win.

The battle lay on one side of a peninsula. Athens was on the other. The city was defenseless, because all its fighting men were at the battle.

The Persian commanders ordered their oarsmen to get to the city before the Athenian troops. If they could do that, the situation would be reversed. They would be inside the city's stout defensive walls, and the Athenians would have to break in to save it.

The Persians knew they were in a race. They knew that the Athenian soldiers would march back to the city as fast they could. They knew that the Athenians didn't have to travel as far as they did. The sea route around the tip of the peninsula and up the other side was nearly seventy miles. The land route was twenty miles. But galleys could travel much faster than marching men, more than ten miles an hour in short bursts.

As they saw the galleys powering away, the Athenian commanders realized the danger they were in. Their men were already tired from fighting in the battle, and some were wounded. Yet there was no time to rest. They had to get going immediately. The Athenians had another handicap: They had to carry their equipment. The gear was cumbersome and heavy—up to seventy pounds per man. Like the Persians, they knew they were in a very desperate race. That knowledge drove them forward. They walked as fast as they could. Some of the more energetic ones would even break into an occasional jog. These jogs wouldn't last long. Their gear was just too heavy.

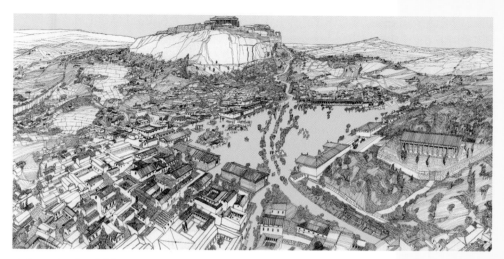

Athens in the fifth century BCE was protected by the sea and a defensive wall (left in picture). If Persia had captured the city in 490 BCE, many of Athens' temples, including the Parthenon (on the hill), would never have been built.

The troops didn't know it, but they were competing in history's first marathon. The morning's battle took place on the Plain of Marathon. A village named Marathon lay a few miles north of the actual fighting. The Persian galleys had landed on the shores of the Bay of Marathon.

The eight thousand Athenians won that first marathon race. When the Persians saw the grim men waiting for them, they knew they had lost. The Persians still outnumbered the Athenians, but soldiers trying to come ashore on a heavily defended beach are at a severe disadvantage. Many Persians would be slaughtered. Their commanders realized they had no chance to capture Athens. They turned around. They had many miles to row before they would reach safety.

Finally the exhausted Athenian warriors could celebrate what they had just accomplished. A relative handful of men had administered a stinging defeat to an army previously thought to be invincible.

Centuries later, a legend would arise from this day. According to the legend, a messenger ran from the battlefield. When he arrived at the gates of the anxiously awaiting city, he gasped, "Rejoice! We conquer!" Then he died from his exertions.

It is very unlikely that this incident happened. Greek messengers were trained to cover much longer distances comfortably. Such a feat had been accomplished just a few days earlier, in fact.

"The Athenian generals sent off a message to Sparta," a famous account says. "The messenger was an Athenian named Pheidippides, a professional long-distance runner. . . . He reached Sparta the day after he left Athens and delivered his message to the Spartan government."[1]

There was good reason for appealing to Sparta. The Spartans were regarded as the best warriors in ancient Greece. Their presence on the battlefield would tilt the odds in the Athenians' favor.

The two cities were about 140 miles apart, so Pheidippides averaged 70 miles each day. He found the Spartans in the midst of an important religious festival. They could come in a week, they said.

Pheidippides immediately began his return journey. For him, running nearly 300 miles was all in a few days' work. It is unlikely that a man capable of running so far and so fast—whether it was the legendary Pheidippides or another professional messenger—would have had any trouble running the twenty miles from the battlefield to Athens.

Nevertheless, the legend persisted. When the Olympic Games were revived in 1896, the European organizers had all studied Greek history and knew about the legend. They decided to have a race to "commemorate" the messenger. The race followed the same route from Marathon to Athens that an ancient messenger would have taken. Appropriately, the winner of the first official marathon was Greek. He didn't have any special training. He didn't die. Nor did any of the other men who had entered. That run was the first modern marathon.

The Battle of Marathon is one of the highlights of another historic first. The account appears in a book called the *Histories*. Scholars consider the book to be the first history. Its author was born a few years after the Battle of Marathon.

His name was Herodotus.

The Hoplites

The men who won at Marathon were called hoplites. The name applied to the infantrymen in any Greek polis. It comes from *hoplon,* the heavy wooden shields the men carried. The shields were three feet across and edged with bronze.

Shields weren't the only protection for hoplites. Bronze shin guards called greaves protected their lower legs. Bronze armor protected their chests. They wore bronze helmets that covered most of the face and the head down to the neck. Their primary weapon was an iron-tipped spear that could be 12 feet long. They also carried swords. The gear for each man weighed between 50 and 70 pounds.

Hoplites provided their own equipment It was expensive. Only reasonably well-to-do men could afford it. Many owned small farms that generated enough income to pay for their gear.

In nearly every polis, being a soldier was a part-time occupation. Campaigning normally occurred only from late spring to early fall. During these campaigns, the troops were arranged in a phalanx, a rectangular formation of wide rows that were usually eight men deep. A phalanx could stretch across a half mile or more.

Hoplites

Each man held his spear in his right hand. His left arm supported the shield. It covered his left side and the right side of the man to his left. His own right side was protected by the man to his right.

In a sense, the phalanx was like a modern-day tank. Instead of guns, an opponent faced a wall of heavy shields that bristled with thousands of spears. Against lightly armored troops such as the Persians, whose shields were made of wicker, the phalanx was an almost irresistible force.

Many poleis engaged in hoplite warfare against one another. Each phalanx would walk toward the other one. At the last moment, they would break into a run. Some men in the front row would be killed on impact. They would immediately be replaced by the men directly behind them. The rest of the men would lean forward and push their shields into the men just ahead of them. Each side tried to push back the other.

The area where they met became a slippery, bloody mush. Normally one side proved stronger in a relatively short time. The losing troops would turn and run away, and the battle would be over.

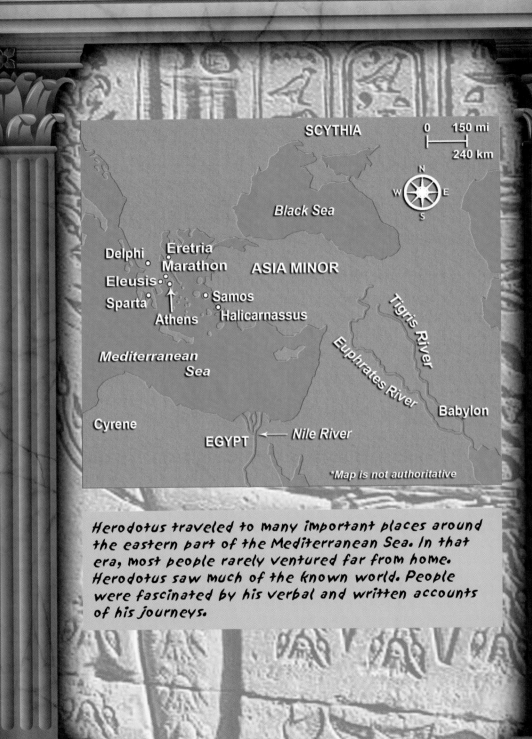

SCYTHIA

0 150 mi

240 km

N W E S

Black Sea

Delphi
Eretria
Marathon   ASIA MINOR
Eleusis
Sparta   Samos
Athens   Halicarnassus

Tigris River

Euphrates River

Mediterranean
Sea

Babylon

Cyrene

EGYPT ← Nile River

*Map is not authoritative

Herodotus traveled to many important places around
the eastern part of the Mediterranean Sea. In that
era, most people rarely ventured far from home.
Herodotus saw much of the known world. People
were fascinated by his verbal and written accounts
of his journeys.

CHAPTER
TWO

SKETCHING A LIFE

Almost nothing is known with absolute certainty about Herodotus' life. The fullest account comes from a manuscript published many centuries after his death. It is less than ten sentences long.

That doesn't mean that Herodotus was obscure. He was very well known during his lifetime. Scholars have located numerous contemporary references to him. The *Histories* also gives many clues.

One thing that seems certain is that he was born in the city of Halicarnassus, one of the Greek-speaking settlements that stretched along the southwest coast of Asia Minor (modern Turkey.) The people in these settlements were known as Ionian Greeks.

It also seems certain that he undertook a series of journeys. These journeys provided him with firsthand knowledge of much of the ancient world. He would use this knowledge in two ways. One was in giving public presentations. In his era, most people never traveled more than a few miles from home. They were fascinated to hear him talk about foreign cultures. The second was in writing *Histories*.

The likely date of his birth is around 484 BCE. His father was Lyxes. His mother was Dryo. An uncle may have been Panyassis, a famous epic poet.

He may have begun his travels when he completed his education at about the age of twenty. At some point, Herodotus had to leave Halicarnassus. He seems to have taken part in a revolt against Lygdamis, the city's ruler. The revolt failed. Panyassis was killed during the uprising.

Scholars believe that Herodotus fled to the island of Samos, another Ionian settlement. His exile there may have served as a training period in research. He carefully recorded his observations of the island and its past. He apparently returned to Halicarnassus as part of another effort to overthrow Lygdamis. This one was successful.

Some commentators suggest that Lygdamis was more popular than the usurpers believed. Herodotus soon realized that he wasn't welcome in Halicarnassus. He had to leave. Others suggest that this overthrow occurred when Herodotus had already completed most of his travels. His public presentations in Halicarnassus flopped. He decided to move to Athens, whose citizens, he felt, would appreciate what he had to offer.

Although Herodotus traveled widely, it is a mistake to think of him as an explorer. He wasn't the type of person to venture into the unknown, but was content to spend much of his time in large cities. When he did venture out, it was usually with merchants or other travelers who were familiar with the territory through which they were passing.

The first of these long trips may have been to Scythia, the region north of the Black Sea in modern-day Ukraine. His most famous journey was to Egypt, where he apparently traveled a great distance up the Nile River. He was familiar with many other regions. He may have gone as far east as ancient Babylon and as far west as Cyrene in Libya.

He probably spent at least a year or two in Athens, one of the most important Greek poleis, or city-states. In 507 BCE it had become the world's first democracy. When Pericles became its leader in 460, he made the city the center of art, architecture, theater, and other cultural pursuits.

For a man of Herodotus' accomplishments, settling in Athens would have made a lot of sense. He couldn't go back to Halicarnassus. He was reputedly a friend of many important Greek thinkers. Some historians date his arrival to sometime around 445 BCE. There are indications that

Born about 495 BCE, Pericles became one of the most important democratically elected leaders in Athens. He was responsible for building many of the temples and other structures that continue to draw tourists to the city today.

an Athenian citizen named Anytus wanted to reward Herodotus for coming to Athens. He proposed a large payment of money to Herodotus that year. Herodotus must have been tempted to settle down there.

But there was a problem. A law passed in Athens in 450 BCE limited citizenship to those whose fathers and mothers were both Athenians. Those who didn't qualify were classified as metics, or resident foreigners. They could live quite comfortably in Athens, but they couldn't become full citizens. They couldn't vote, and they couldn't own land.

The solution to Herodotus' dilemma lay to the west. A number of Greek poleis established colonies. Many were in Italy. One of these was Thurii. The new settlement would have allowed him the privileges of full citizenship and the opportunity to own land. It is likely that he moved there soon after the colony was founded in 443 BCE. It's also likely that he wrote most, if not all, of the *Histories* in Thurii.

He probably was alive in 431 BCE when the Peloponnesian War broke out. The primary combatants were Athens and Sparta. Many poleis supported one side or the other. For the Greeks, it was a miniature world war. Almost certainly Herodotus died long before it ended in 404 BCE. Most commentators place the date of his death about twenty years earlier. No one knows where he died, though Thurii is the most likely site.

In modern times, people study many different branches of knowledge: history, science, and literature, for example. In turn, each branch is subdivided: science includes subjects such as chemistry, biology, and physics. Each of these subjects is carved up even further: astrophysics, biophysics, atomic physics, and so on.

In Herodotus' time, there were no such divisions. *History* meant "inquiry" or "investigation." His *Histories* contains elements beyond just recounting events, including geography, literature, science, mythology, and much more.

In numerous cases, these elements seem to be fictional. Herodotus has been criticized by modern scholars (and some ancient ones as well) for his lack of accuracy. He seems to have always enjoyed a good story. While he probably didn't make things up completely, more than likely he listened to many stories people (mostly local people) told him, and recorded the marvels he saw. At that time, it was often difficult to cross-check those stories for accuracy.

Those stories would have been one reason that his lectures (at least in Athens) were so popular. Herodotus probably knew that he could spend the rest of his life serving as a well-paid public entertainer. It wasn't enough for him.

At some point, he made a momentous decision. He must have been an ambitious man. He wanted to leave something of himself behind. He wouldn't abandon his lively stories. He would give them a focus, an overall plan.

The Ionian Greeks

FYI For Your Info

The "modern" era of ancient Greece is dated from about 800 BCE. That is when self-contained city-states began to emerge. Called poleis, they consisted of a central town and the surrounding countryside. Each polis wasn't very large. The Greek landscape—with many mountains and valleys—naturally divided the country into small regions. Because Greek soil is not especially fertile, each polis could support only a certain number of inhabitants.

Many poleis grew to have more people than they could support. They encouraged some of their people to move away. The southwestern coast of modern-day Turkey provided some logical sites. Some Greeks were already there, having fled earlier invasions from the north. Their legendary leader was Ion. As a result, the rapidly growing settlement area became known as Ionia.

Ionia lay along a coastal stretch of about 100 miles. It included ten major cities and two islands (Samos and Chios) that lay just offshore. Ionia became very important in the rise of Greek culture. The famous poet Homer grew up in Ionia. Ionian thinkers, especially those in the city of Miletus, developed many important ideas.

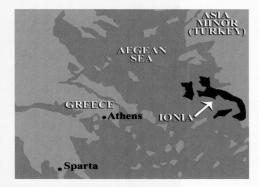

The Ionian colonists were very similar to their fellow Greeks in their religious beliefs. Politically they were independent—at least in the beginning. In the mid-500s BCE, a foreign ruler named Croesus conquered them. In turn, the Persian King Cyrus defeated Croesus. That brought the Ionians under Persian control. This Persian control ended in 479 BCE with the Battle of Plataea.

The Ionian cities continued to grow and thrive, establishing a permanent Greek presence in Turkey. Two thousand years later, Turkey reached across the Aegean and took over all of Greece. The ruling Turks and the conquered Greeks hated each other. The hatred erupted into open war in 1821 CE. With the aid of several foreign powers, Greece gained its independence from Turkey. The enmity between the two countries continued. After World War I, Greece occupied Turkey. The Turks fought back and defeated the Greeks in 1922. The survivors fled to Greece. Three millennia of Greek settlements in Turkey came to an end.

ΗΡΟΔΟΤΟC

The inscription on this bust leaves no doubt that it is Herodotus. However, some of the Greek letters are different from the Roman alphabet. For example, the H is pronounced as E, the P as R, and the C at the end as S.

CHAPTER
THREE

THE WORLD ACCORDING TO HERODOTUS

In *Histories*, Herodotus decided to show the origins of the Persian War. When the Greeks defeated the Persians, they regarded it as one of the most important events in their history. The victory allowed them the freedom to maintain their way of life. "Such is our love of freedom, that we will defend ourselves in any way we can,"[1] Herodotus noted.

To research his work, Herodotus embarked on a new round of travels, this time throughout Greece. He examined battlefields and monuments, and he talked to men who had fought in the conflict. There probably weren't many left. Even the youngest veteran of Marathon would have been in his late sixties. At that time, relatively few people lived that long.

Why would he undertake such an ambitious project? According to one theory, he foresaw the chaos that the Greek community was about to sink into. The differences between Athens and Sparta were increasing. The two sides had already come to blows on several occasions. Herodotus knew the situation could easily turn more violent.

According to this theory, he wanted to remind the two sides about what they had in common: the glory of their working together in order to defeat the Persians.

In modern times, many commentators refer to the men and women who fought in World War II—after first surviving the Great Depression—as the Greatest Generation. Perhaps Herodotus felt the same way about the men who had stood in the path of the Persian invasion. They preserved the freedoms of the Greeks. They put aside their differences in favor of the greater good.

Unfortunately, Herodotus failed to prevent the civil war that shredded Greece. His successor Thucydides would vividly describe the long nightmare that soon descended on the Greek landscape.

To many people today, Athens has the reputation of being the ideal ancient city. It was a democracy. It was the center of Greek culture. Its enduring symbol was the Parthenon, a temple dedicated to the goddess Athena. An architectural marvel, the Parthenon is one of the most famous buildings ever constructed.

Yet Athens didn't enjoy this reputation among its peers. Many Greek poleis resented the way that Athens treated them after the Persian War. For example, the city had formed the Delian League. Its purpose was to defend against the possibility of another Persian invasion. It was founded on a simple principle: All its members would be equal, and they would all contribute money. The money would be used to benefit *all* the members.

It didn't take long for Athens to control the Delian League, which angered the other poleis. Then Athenians moved the League's treasury to their city. Sometimes they used the money for their own purposes.

Athens became very ambitious. The city's leaders wanted to form an empire. That was fine with Athens, but not with much of the rest of the Greek world.

Herodotus may also have been trying to show the Athenians the dangers of their imperial ambitions. He starts the *Histories* with a discussion of the origins of the Persian Empire. He saw ominous parallels between those origins and what Athens was doing. He thoroughly approved of the Greek victory over the Persians. His point was that Persia had become too ambitious, too greedy, and that had led to their defeat. He didn't want Athens to fall into the same trap.

The Parthenon is one of the most famous structures in Athens. Building began in 447 BCE, around the time Herodotus was living in the city.

The book begins: "Herodotus of Halicarnassus here displays his history [meaning "inquiry"], so that human achievements may not become forgotten in time, and great and marvelous deeds—some displayed by Greeks, some by barbarians—may not be without their glory; and especially to show why the two peoples [Greeks and Persians] fought with each other."[2]

By "barbarian," Herodotus and other Greeks didn't mean people who lived under primitive conditions. Rather, *barbarian* was a general term for anyone who didn't speak Greek. To a Greek, foreign languages and even a few of the more remote Greek dialects all sounded like "bar-bar-bar."

Herodotus may have been eager to showcase the "great and marvelous deeds" of both sides because of his birthplace. In Halicarnassus, he had been exposed to many cultures, including Persian. In most cases, he tried to give a balanced presentation.

"[Herodotus] refused to demonize the Greeks' opponents, and instead represented them as multifaceted individuals combining both admirable and repellent characteristics. On the other side, there is a consistent strain of criticism throughout the work of Greek ways and institutions," says classics professor John Marincola. "At the very end of the *Histories*, it looks as if the Athenians are becoming the new aggressors, taking on the characteristics of the barbarians they have just defeated."[3]

This approach is very different from modern-day attitudes, which often "demonize" opposing countries. For example, in 2002, U.S. President George W. Bush referred to Iran as part of the "Axis of Evil." The Iranians replied that the United States was the "Great Satan."

Although Herodotus was writing about an old war, the Greeks didn't consider the story to be old news. As J.A.S. Evans, another classics professor, notes, "By the time Herodotus wrote, the Persian War had become, in Greek minds, part of a long struggle between Greek and barbarian that went back at least to the Trojan War."[4]

Herodotus begins his *Histories* with a brief examination of the Trojan War. He shows that both sides had legitimate grievances in the conflict. These mutual grievances continued for several centuries, so he skips ahead to the century before his own. He looks for someone who clearly wronged the Greeks. In his mind, this "someone" was Croesus of Lydia. He wasn't the first ruler to lead an attack against the Greeks, but he was the first to attack them and then impose tribute after his victory. Paying tribute became the mark of an empire.

The story of Croesus serves as an early example of the way Herodotus operates. Herodotus provides a great deal of information about Croesus and how he came to power. He gives the history through stories that people told him during his wanderings.

Croesus soon felt threatened by Cyrus, the Persian king, whose empire lay to the east. Croesus wondered if he should invade part of that empire. To find out, he sent an envoy to the ancient oracle at Delphi. Oracles held a unique place in the ancient world. They issued predictions, though they were sometimes hard to understand. The oracle's message was satisfying to Croesus. It told him that he would destroy a great empire.

Croesus launched an attack, but Cyrus defeated him in battle. Croesus sent an angry message to the oracle, complaining that he had been given a bad prophecy. The oracle replied that the prophecy had been correct. A great empire *had* been destroyed. The empire was his own.

With Croesus gone, the Persian Empire became the greatest threat to the Greeks. Characteristically, Herodotus spends a great deal of time discussing Cyrus and his ancestors. Then he details each of Cyrus's conquests: each country's history, culture, and customs.

Eventually Cyrus meets his end in battle. He is succeeded by Cambyses, his son, who decides to invade Egypt. This sets up the book's longest digression. At its beginning, Herodotus writes, "About Egypt I shall have a great deal more to relate because of the number of remarkable things which the country contains, and because of the fact that more monuments. . . are to be found there than anywhere else in the world."[5]

When he relies on direct observation, there seems little doubt that he accurately records actual conditions. For example, he notes, "The Egyptians themselves in their manners and customs seem to have reversed the ordinary practices of mankind. Women attend market and are employed in trade, while men stay at home and do the weaving."[6]

His Athenian audience must have gasped in disbelief. Women in Athens had two primary purposes: bearing children and taking care of the household. They rarely appeared in public.

The truth of other passages seems more dubious. For example, he describes the process of "gold mining" in a desert in India. India was the most populous province in the Persian Empire.

"There is found in this desert a kind of ant of great size—bigger than a fox, though not so big as a dog," Herodotus begins. "These creatures as they burrow underground throw up the sand in heaps. . . . The sand has a rich content of gold, and this it is what the Indians are after when they make their expeditions into the desert."[7]

The prospectors carefully time their arrival for the hottest part of the day. The blazing sun drives the ants deep underground. The men quickly shovel the mounds of gold-laden sand into bags. They load the heavy bags onto their camels. Then they "start for home again as fast as they can go; for the ants . . . smell them and at once give chase; nothing in the world can touch these ants for speed, so not one of the Indians would get home alive, if they did not make sure of a good start while the ants were mustering their forces."[8]

Herodotus finally returns to his main narrative. Cambyses has gone insane, and Darius succeeds him. Herodotus details several military campaigns led by Darius. These campaigns end about halfway through the *Histories*. At this point he sets the stage for the epic confrontation between the Persians and the Greeks.

In 499 BCE, the Ionian Greeks rose in revolt. At first the revolt was successful. Athens helped by sending troops to support the rebels. So did Eretria, a city on the island of Euboea. The high point came with the burning of the Persian provincial capital of Sardis. But the Persians were too powerful, and the revolt was defeated in 494. The Ionians returned to Persian control.

Darius was outraged when he learned that Athens and Eretria had supported the Ionians. He swore revenge.

There seemed little doubt that he would get it.

The Delphic Oracle

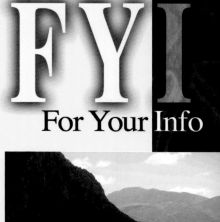

For Your Info

The Delphic Oracle was the most important place of prophecy in the ancient world. The Greeks believed the oracle lay at the center of the world. It was built around a stone called the omphalos, meaning "navel." The Greeks considered the omphalos to be the navel of the earth.

The site, located on the slope of Mt. Parnassus, was believed to be sacred to the god Apollo. People came from hundreds of miles away to consult it. Their concerns ranged from the very personal to events that could shape the destinies of millions of people.

Temple ruins at Delphi

The woman who made the actual prophecies was called the Pythia. People approached her by walking up the Sacred Way, a zigzag path lined with statues and treasuries. Treasuries were tiny temples. Poleis erected them to reward the Pythia for prophecies that favored them.

When they arrived at the temple, people sacrificed a sheep or goat, then entered a small room under the temple. The Pythia sat on a small chair over an opening in the earth. She listened to her visitors, then she gave her prophecy. Many of her predictions were not very clear. They were based on visions she had.

Recent research has revealed one possible source of her visions. Two small cracks in the earth's crust intersect beneath the temple. These cracks allowed hallucinogenic gases to seep upward. In an enclosed room, the gases would become concentrated. They wouldn't be fatal, but they would make a person who breathed them over an extended period of time have visions.

Scholars estimate that the oracle dates from 1200 BCE. The site was active until just before 400 CE. By that time, the Christian religion had become dominant in the Mediterranean. Few people were interested in pagan gods such as Apollo.

In modern times, the Delphic Oracle has reopened. Throngs of people pack it every day. A handful may be in search of wisdom. For the rest, it's a chance to visit one of the most important ancient sites. In addition to the temple, there's also an athletic stadium, a theater, and a museum that displays Delphi's priceless treasures.

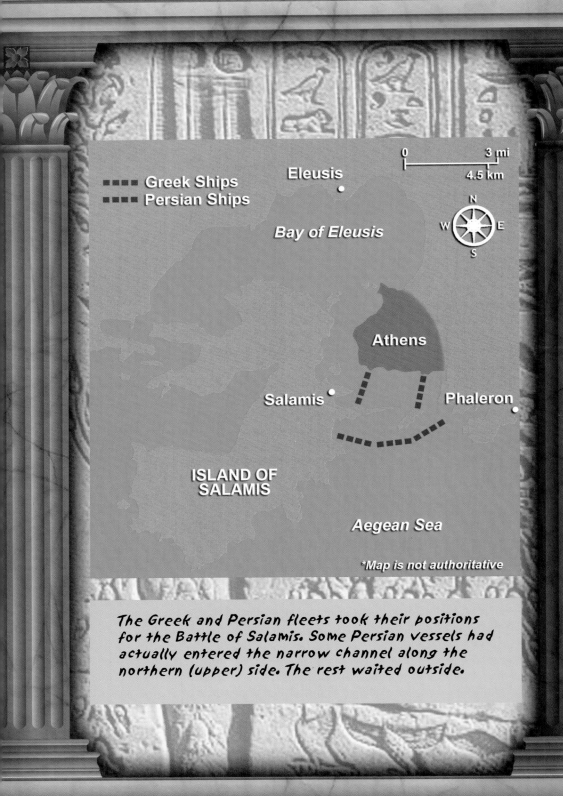

Greek Ships
Persian Ships

0   3 mi
4.5 km

N
W   E
S

Eleusis

Bay of Eleusis

Athens

Salamis

Phaleron

ISLAND OF
SALAMIS

Aegean Sea

*Map is not authoritative

The Greek and Persian fleets took their positions
for the Battle of Salamis. Some Persian vessels had
actually entered the narrow channel along the
northern (upper) side. The rest waited outside.

CHAPTER
FOUR

JOLTING THE PERSIAN JUGGERNAUT

In 490 BCE, four years after the Ionian revolt was squelched, Darius sent Datis, a general, and about 30,000 troops to exact his vengeance. Eretria was the first stop. After a weeklong resistance, some of the city's leaders betrayed it. The inhabitants were enslaved.

Then it was the Athenians' turn. The Persians rowed into Marathon Bay. The bay had miles of long, sandy beaches. Few ripples disturbed the surface of the water. The Athenian troops gathered on a hill overlooking the bay and the Plain of Marathon. Their position blocked the one road that led to Athens.

The two sides spent a week staring at each other. Seeking help Pheidippides made his legendary run to Sparta. The Athenian high command was divided. Some wanted to fight. Some didn't. Finally they made up their minds. They decided on a desperate strategy. Normally they fought in three approximately equal wings: left, center, and right. This time they chose to deliberately weaken their center. The two outer wings would be much stronger.

The plan worked. Datis had placed his best troops in the center. They easily pushed back the Athenians there. It was a different story on the wings. The Athenians quickly cut down their enemies. The survivors fled.

The Athenians didn't pursue them. Instead, they wheeled inward and formed a solid line of men. Then they rushed to help their comrades in the center. Moments earlier, the Persians there had rejoiced over their apparent victory. Now they realized they were surrounded. They panicked. Many threw down their weapons. Those who could rushed to their ships. Then the ships headed for Athens. They arrived too late.

It was a shining moment in Greek history. As Herodotus notes, the Athenians who fought at Marathon were "the first who dared to look without flinching at Persian dress and the men who wore it; for until that day came, no Greek could hear even the name Persian without terror."[1]

Darius was furious. "When the news of the battle of Marathon reached Darius," Herodotus continues, "his anger against Athens . . . was even greater, and he was more than ever determined to make war on Greece."[2] Darius regarded this failure as simply Round One. He decided that Round Two would be the knockout blow. He began assembling a much larger army.

A revolt in Egypt gave the Greeks a break. Darius dealt with the Egyptians first. He died in 486 in a battle. His son and successor, Xerxes I, however, didn't miss a beat. He immediately took up the cause—and it wasn't just against Athens. Already in control of much of northern Greece, Xerxes believed that he could conquer the rest of the Greek poleis.

It was a massive undertaking. He had to stockpile caches of food, build roads, and figure out how to cross rivers and other bodies of water. Preparations took three years. In 481, they were complete. He assembled a juggernaut, a massive force that would crush anything it encountered. Herodotus says it numbered nearly 2,000,000 men. This figure is almost certainly incorrect. It would be very difficult to supply an army that large even in modern times. A figure of about 250,000 is much more likely and would still have greatly outnumbered the Greek soldiers. Another force of about the same size manned Xerxes' ships. Because Persia was a land power, his fleet of well over 1,000 fighting ships came from its subject states: Phoenicia, Egypt, even the Ionian Greek colonies.

Despite their obvious differences in government, Sparta and Athens had two things in common: They were free because of their respect for law, and neither the Spartans nor the Athenians had any intention of being ruled at the whim of an emperor.

Many poleis didn't share that outlook. As Xerxes advanced into Greece, many of them chose to yield to his authority. They provided him with even more soldiers. The Persian strategy was obvious. First they would destroy Athens. Then they would continue into Peloponnesia, a large peninsula west of Athens, where Sparta was located. They would overwhelm the Spartans, which would probably end the war. No other poleis had the strength of Athens or Sparta. Xerxes felt very confident about his strategy.

He hit a momentary roadblock at the narrow pass of Thermopylae, located about forty miles north of Athens. The sea lay on one side. A very high cliff lay on the other. A force of three hundred Spartan warriors provided the primary defense. A few thousand other Greeks supported them. The Spartans knew they were unlikely to return. They had been chosen to defend Thermopylae because they all had sons to keep their family name alive.

They fought ferociously for two days, repelling wave after wave of onslaughts. They killed thousands of Persians before they were betrayed. A man showed the Persians a secret path, over the cliff and behind the pass. The Spartans knew they were doomed. They sent the other Greeks away and made their last stand. All three hundred were killed. The last ones to die fought with their fists and teeth.

Now the Persians had a clear route to Athens. The frightened citizens fled. Most of them slipped across a narrow strait to the island of Salamis. The Greek triremes, the leading fighting vessels of the ancient world, were already there. Athens was almost a ghost town. Only a few fanatics remained. The onlookers on Salamis had a bitter sight. The Persians torched their beloved city and much of the surrounding countryside.

This desperate situation led to the Battle of Salamis. Herodotus devotes a considerable portion of his manuscript to the events leading up to the battle and to the battle itself. He and his fellow Greeks knew the vital role that the battle played in Greek history. Many modern historians go further. They believe that Salamis was important not just in Greek history, but in the history of the world.

Herodotus had no doubts about who was most responsible for the battle's successful outcome: "One is surely right in saying that Greece was saved by the Athenians."[3]

The Athenians faced a crucial decision. They could submit to Xerxes. They could flee. Or they could stand and fight.

It took a great deal of courage not to choose one of those first two options. Their courage was tested even further when they consulted the oracle of Delphi. They were appalled by the reply. "Why sit you, doomed ones? Fly to the world's ends," it began. "Bow your hearts to grief."[4]

This prophecy was so horrifying that a priest associated with the oracle suggested a do-over. He advised the Athenians to approach the oracle with olive branches and ask for something better.

The new prophecy didn't sound like much of an improvement: "The wooden wall only shall not fall, but help you and your children. But await not the host of horse and foot coming from Asia, not be still but turn your back and withdraw from the foe. . . . Divine Salamis, you will bring death to women's sons when the corn is scattered, or the harvest gathered in."[5]

Most people thought that the "wooden wall" meant the defenses surrounding Athens. To them, this new advice was contradictory: Stay behind the wall, and yet go.

A few took a less literal approach. The "wooden wall" was actually the hulls of their ships. Yet they too were discouraged. The last line suggested that they would lose a naval battle off the island of Salamis.

One man, an Athenian general named Themistocles, was much more upbeat. Several years earlier, a rich deposit of silver had been discovered near Athens. The Athenians wanted to use the money for themselves. Themistocles believed that the money could be put to better use. He convinced the Athenians to spend the windfall on ships. The Greek fleet at Salamis was all that stood between Xerxes and his goal. Most of the ships were Athenian—the very ones that had been built with the silver.

Themistocles used his speaking skills to boost the morale of the Greeks. He pointed out that the oracle had used the phrase "divine Salamis." If the oracle were prophesying doom, he said, she would have used a word such as "hateful." Therefore, the "women's sons" to whom death would come were the Persians.

Arguing about words didn't change one essential fact. Two storms and a battle not far from Thermopylae had reduced the Persian fleet to nearly half. Yet they still had more than 600 triremes. The Greeks had just over 300. They were still greatly outnumbered.

Themistocles was under another handicap. He wasn't in overall command. A Spartan named Eurybiades was. Because the alliance among the various poleis wasn't strong, everyone agreed that Sparta was the Greeks' most important military power. That reputation was based mostly on their army. None of them—including Eurybiades—knew much about naval warfare, yet they insisted on holding supreme power at sea as well. His appointment showed how desperate the Athenians were. To hold the alliance together, they were willing to let a landlubber command their warships.

Still, there were bitter quarrels among the Greek commanders. They held a council of war over whether they should try to defend Salamis. If they fought the Persians there and lost, they would join the Athenian civilians and be trapped. If they fought elsewhere and lost, they could still go ashore and make their escape. The council decided to hoist anchor and abandon Athens. Themistocles tried to change their minds. He failed.

Most of the commanders headed for their ships. They couldn't wait to board and sail away. In one final effort, Themistocles sat down with Eurybiades. He mentioned the sacrifice of the Spartans at Thermopylae. They had given their lives to keep the Greeks—not just the Spartans— free. Bailing out now would insult their sacrifice. Besides, Themistocles said, he had a plan. He would convert the Greeks' weakness in numbers into a strength. Then he played his trump card. He said that if the other commanders abandoned him, he would take the Athenian ships and abandon *them*. The Athenian fleet would carry the citizens to southern Italy. They would establish a new colony. They would survive. Without the Athenian fleet, the other Greeks would be helpless. They would perish.

Eurybiades bought into Themistocles' plan. So did the other Greek commanders. There was no longer any talk among the Greeks of leaving the Athenians to their fate.

One obstacle remained. The success of Themistocles' plan depended entirely on the Persians acting in precisely the way that he wanted them to. How could he make sure they would?

It was late September, and Xerxes needed to complete his campaign. The Persians had picked the landscape around Athens clean of anything to eat. Now they were dependent on a steady stream of supply ships. The Aegean Sea is notoriously stormy during the late fall and winter. The approaching bad weather would deprive Xerxes of those supplies.

Xerxes was eager to force the Greeks into a decisive battle. The Persians had spies. They knew about the quarrels among the Greeks. Xerxes took advantage of this knowledge. He ordered the army to start marching out of Athens toward Sparta. They deliberately made as much noise as possible. He wanted the Greeks to hear his advance. He hoped that they would send part of the fleet to help defend Sparta. If that happened, his navy could easily defeat the Athenians, then mop up the remnants of the Greek fleet.

He ordered the navy to make its preparations. They would go into action against what he believed would be a diminished Greek fleet the following day. Then he went to bed. He felt confident that in the morning, he would complete his father's ten-year quest.

He didn't sleep very long. His generals woke him with explosive news. The Greeks were running away!

There had been yet another change of heart. The non-Athenian Greeks had had a full day to think about the reversal of their earlier desire to flee. They decided their original decision had been the best.

This news came from a Greek deserter named Sinnicus. He had stolen away from Salamis and rowed to Phaleron, the beach near Athens where Persian ships were moored. He was ushered to the generals who commanded the fleet. No one knows how long it took him to convince them that his news was true, but one thing is certain: He was persuasive.

Xerxes, the much feared Persian king, adorned himself with precious metals. Even on war campaigns, he kept up kingly appearances. He ate fancy meals on gold and silver tables in a huge, lavishly decorated tent. His horses wore golden bridles and ate from a bronze manger. As his men fought their battles, Xerxes would watch from a golden throne.

Phaleron was several miles from Salamis. Xerxes knew there was no time to lose. His ships were lighter and faster than those of the Greeks. If he waited, the Greeks would have too much of a head start. They would escape. Xerxes ordered his ships to leave right away, even though it was still very early in the morning. The skies were completely dark. Some of his ships penetrated up to two miles into the Salamis Channel next to the mainland. That cut off the Greeks' escape route.

The Persians were confident that their superior numbers and speed would result in a decisive victory. The final obstacle to the complete conquest of Greece would be removed. Xerxes probably was too excited to go back to sleep. He would have been even more restless if he knew for whom Sinnicus worked.

It was Themistocles. Sinnicus' story made sure that Themistocles had everything he had hoped for.

When the Greeks woke up that morning, they saw they were almost completely surrounded. Flight was no longer an option. They had to fight. And the fight would take place exactly where Themistocles wanted it to.

At dawn, Xerxes' servants set up a golden throne on a hill overlooking the channel. Their master wanted to witness the crushing of the last hope of the Greeks. Instead, he witnessed his navy blundering into a trap.

Themistocles had chosen his ground carefully. Only part of the Persian fleet could fit into the narrow channel. The rest had to wait outside. That removed their overall edge in numbers. The channel also provided a conduit for the southerly wind that normally began blowing in midmorning. The wind kicked up the waves. The heavier Greek ships were fairly stable in these sea conditions, but some Persian ships became almost uncontrollable. They were blown about and became more vulnerable to the heavy rams of the Greeks.

Rams, the main weapon of ancient warships, were attached to the bow. They extended forward by as much as eight or ten feet. The added weight of the Greek ships increased the strength of their blows as they smashed into the Persian vessels.

The Persians were at a great disadvantage for other reasons. They had been awake all night. As the day grew hotter, everyone became fatigued. Fatigue affected the sleepless Persians more than the Greeks.

The Persian command structure was very rigid. Losing their leaders had a serious effect. Subordinate units would become confused and unsure of what to do. The Greeks were much more flexible. If a leader went down, his followers were comfortable continuing without him.

Finally, the Persians believed that they would be facing a demoralized enemy that was on the run. Instead, the Greeks attacked *them*. As Strauss notes, "The Greeks on Salamis unleashed the storm of war on an enemy that had expected a drizzle."[6]

Themistocles was aware of all these factors. The battle soon swung in the Greeks' favor. Some of the Persian ships tried to get out of what seemed like a death trap. Their retreat gave the Greeks another advantage.

The ships lying outside the channel could hear the sounds of the battle. From their vantage point, they couldn't see what was happening. Many began advancing into the channel. There they met the retreating ships. In the chaos, it became virtually impossible to maneuver.

More and more Persian ships were rammed. Some sank. Others became waterlogged hulks that only added to the logjam. Many, if not most, lost their entire crews. Some men drowned in the wreckage of their ships. Others managed to scramble overboard. Herodotus maintains that most Persian oarsmen couldn't swim and quickly went under. The ones who could, and the ones who clung to pieces of wreckage, lived a little longer. Their own fleeing ships didn't take the time to stop and pick them up. The enemy ships didn't either. The Greeks slew them with arrows. Some Persians floundered ashore on Salamis. The Greeks killed them too. Finally the shattered Persian fleet managed to flee to Phaleron. They left behind an estimated 40,000 dead men.

Herodotus approved of the Greek victory, yet he couldn't resist recording a certain amount of hometown pride. He may have thoroughly disliked Lygdamis, the king against whom he had twice revolted. He held a very different opinion about Lygdamis' grandmother, Artemisia. Even though she fought on the side of the Persians, her exploits reflected favorably on Halicarnassus. She had five galleys under her command.

"It seems a marvel that she—a woman—should have taken part in the campaign against Greece," he wrote. "On the death of her husband the tyranny had passed into her hands, and she sailed with the fleet in spite of the fact that she had a grown-up son and that there was consequently no necessity for her to do so. Her own spirit of adventure and manly courage were her only incentives."[7]

It was rare enough for a woman to rule in the ancient world. It was almost unheard of for one to command a military unit.

During the battle, Aminias, one of the most successful Greek captains, bore down on her ship. She couldn't flee. Instead, she quickly turned her ship and attacked another Persian vessel. She sank it. Then she made sure there were no survivors to spread the tale of her treachery.

The grim episode had two benefits. It made Aminias think that Artemisia was on his side. He turned away to go after other targets. Even more important, it impressed Xerxes. On a day when few things were going right, Artemisia's "victory" seemed to be a bright spot.

"Xerxes asked if [his servants] were sure it was really Artemisia, and was told that there was no doubt whatever—they knew her ensign [flag] well, and of course supposed that it was an enemy ship that had been sunk," Herodotus wrote. "Xerxes' comment on what was told him is said to have been: 'My men have turned into women, my women into men.'"[8]

Surveying the carnage, Xerxes wasn't sure about his next step. He knew he couldn't keep his entire force in Greece. There wasn't enough food. His commander in chief, Mardonius, suggested that Xerxes should go home with the bulk of the army and the remaining ships. Mardonius would remain behind with a sizable force and renew the campaign in the spring. Because Xerxes respected Artemisia's judgment, he asked for her opinion.

"If his design prospers, and success attends his arms, it will be *your* work, master," she purred. "Who cares if Mardonius comes to grief? He is only your slave, and the Greeks will have but a poor triumph if they kill him. As for yourself, you will be going home with the object of your campaign accomplished—for you have burnt Athens."[9]

Artemisia conveniently blurred an important fact. Burning Athens *wasn't* the object of the campaign. Conquering Greece was the object. But Artemisia knew her man. As Herodotus notes (probably with some degree of sarcasm), "It was the expression of his own thoughts. Personally, I do not think he would have stayed in Greece, had all his counselors, men and women alike, urged him to do so—he was much too badly frightened."[10]

The idea that the leader of the mightiest power in the western world had been a coward would have greatly appealed to Herodotus' Greek audience. They knew their leaders had been brave.

Mardonius stayed. The following spring, he met a combined force of Greeks at the Battle of Plataea. He was defeated. About the same time, the Greeks won another important battle on the Ionian coast at Mycale.

The Persian War was over, and so was the *Histories*.

Triremes

Triremes were the battleships of their era. Their name comes from the three (*tri-*) banks of rowers on each side. Each bank had about 30 men, so in all, about 180 men propelled the ship. The main challenge was to make sure that they rowed in unison. A rowing master offered overall direction. He stationed a man at each end of the ship to provide the cadence to the oarsmen. The captain, the helmsman, and about 15 fighting men rounded out the crew. They all worked toward a single purpose: to drive their ram into an enemy ship. Even a hole about a foot square would admit hundreds of gallons of seawater every minute.

Triremes

Nearly all the rowers in each ship were citizens of one particular polis. Their personal incomes were relatively low. They couldn't afford the expensive equipment of a hoplite. Serving in a trireme allowed them to help with the defense of their city-state.

Scholars believe that the vessels were about 130 feet long and slightly less than 20 feet wide. They weren't very stable or seaworthy. Their primary hazard (besides battle) was getting caught in the open sea during a sudden storm. As a result, triremes normally stayed as close to shore as they could. It was customary to come ashore during the hottest part of the day for a brief rest and at night to sleep.

Pulling an oar was hard work. The men had to eat a great deal to keep up their strength. They each probably drank up to two gallons of water a day. The deck protected the rowers from the effects of direct sunlight and from enemy arrows. On the other hand, it cut down on ventilation. The air would have become very hot and stifling.

The stench must have been terrible. The confined space held the odors of 180 men who were constantly sweating. There were other smells. Sometimes rowers would vomit. Sometimes they would urinate. There were no bathroom breaks. It would have been especially uncomfortable for the rowers on the lowest level, where these fluids would often drip down.

Herodotus reads the stories of his numerous adventures. In his era, there weren't many public forms of entertainment. People were willing to stand for hours to learn about distant and exotic cultures.

CHAPTER
FIVE

AFTER HERODOTUS

The histories of Herodotus did not prevent the brewing civil war. Another historian, Thucydides, wrote an account of what happened called *History of the Peloponnesian War*. Thucydides didn't think much of Herodotus. He didn't have any qualms about expressing his feelings.

He says early in his book: "With regard to my factual reporting of the events of the war I have made it a principle not to write down the first story that came my way, and not even to be guided by my general impressions; either I was present myself at the events which I have described or else I heard of them from eye-witnesses whose reports I have checked with as much thoroughness as possible. . . . My work is not a piece of writing designed to meet the taste of an immediate public, but was done to last for ever."[1] His comments are an obvious slam at Herodotus.

Thucydides' low opinion of Herodotus became fairly commonplace in the ancient world. Herodotus became known as the father of lies. Even the Roman writer Cicero—who gave him the title of "father of history" in about 50 BCE—criticized him for using so many legends.

For centuries, these "legends" downgraded his reputation—at least among scholars. Even so, he remained one of the most popular of the

An archaeologist works on a newly discovered mummy in Egypt. His research, coupled with the discoveries of many other archaeologists, has given scholars a new appreciation of the marvels that Herodotus described.

ancient Greek writers. According to one estimate, there were actually more editions of the *Histories* produced between 1450 and 1700 than of Thucydides' *History of the Peloponnesian War*. One reason for his ongoing popularity, especially during this period, was renewed interest in remote parts of the world. His colorful tales satisfied this new curiosity.

Thucydides' somewhat spiteful dismissal of Herodotus was clearly in error. Like his own work, Herodotus' work has also lasted "for ever." Many people—classical scholars, students, and ordinary readers—still enjoy Herodotus' descriptions of a world that has long since vanished from sight. His words bring it back to life.

More recently, his reputation has undergone a major upgrade. While some stories—such as the one about the giant ants—are clearly not true, many scholars now believe that Herodotus was essentially correct in the major outlines of his story. As classical historian J.A.S. Evans notes, "As the archaeology of Egypt, Persia, and Assyria became better known, it grew clear that Herodotus's marvelous tales were not imaginary. Our own century has developed a lively respect for him as a reporter. . . . It is unlikely that we shall ever have enough evidence to end this controversy, but Herodotus has emerged from it with a heightened reputation as a researcher."[2]

Barry Strauss agrees. "Herodotus was an excellent historian," he writes. "He was one of the shrewdest and most skeptical students of the past who ever wrote, and also one of the most honest. After decades of being dismissed as a lightweight, Herodotus has of late been appreciated again, as a savvy and mainly reliable historian."[3]

Some of Herodotus' conclusions seem true today. He writes: "Athens went from strength to strength, and proved, if proof was needed, how noble a thing equality before the law is, not in one respect only, but in all; for while they were oppressed under tyrants, they had no better success in war than any of their neighbors, yet, once the yoke was flung off, they proved the finest fighters in the world. This clearly shows that, as long as they were held down by authority, they deliberately shirked their duty in the field, as slaves shirk working for their masters; but when freedom was won, then every man amongst them was interested in his own cause."[4] In other words, free men make better soldiers than slaves do.

A number of people have accused Herodotus of glorifying war. He himself refutes this. "No one is fool enough to choose war instead of peace," he comments. "In peace sons bury fathers, but in war fathers bury sons."[5]

Herodotus illustrates the folly and futility of war. In his *Histories*, he speaks directly to one of the central issues that has plagued human beings for millennia.

Thucydides and the Peloponnesian War

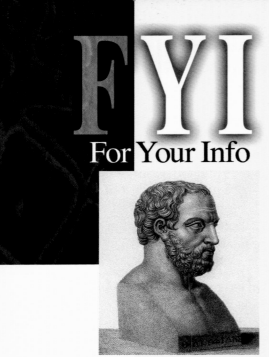

Thucydides

Thucydides was probably born about 460 BCE. He was therefore an adult during the Peloponnesian War. When the war broke out, he commanded a squadron of Athenian ships. Due to circumstances beyond his control, he arrived late for a battle. The Athenians didn't forgive him. They forced him into exile (423–404 BCE). He commented that being exiled allowed him to travel freely on the other side. These travels helped him remain objective in his account of the war.

When open war broke out in 431, a storm between Athens and Sparta had been brewing for decades. Many poleis entered the conflict in support of the primary powers, and Greece found itself in a civil war.

The Athenian leader, Pericles, was confident of victory. The city was linked to its port of Piraeus by impregnable walls. The citizens would be safe inside the walls. Their ships would provide plenty of supplies. In the meantime, the Athenian fleet would take the fight to the enemy. They could land troops anywhere they wanted. Pericles foresaw a short war.

His plan took a major hit almost immediately. A mysterious plague struck the city. Thousands of people died, including Pericles. Despite the setback, the Athenians fought on relatively even terms for about ten years. Then in 421 BCE, the two sides agreed to a thirty-year truce.

The Athenians broke the truce when they invaded Syracuse, the Spartans' main source of supplies, in 414. Cut those supplies off, the Athenians reasoned, and the Spartans would have to give up.

The strategy backfired. The Athenians suffered a catastrophic defeat at Syracuse the following year. Both their army and their navy were virtually destroyed. Somehow they managed to hang on. They even won several minor victories over the next few years. The victories only prolonged their agony. They were forced to surrender to Sparta in 404 BCE.

It is likely that Thucydides died a few years later, probably in 401 or 400. His manuscript wasn't finished. It breaks off in 411, seven years before the end of the war. Ironically, the final episode details a morale-boosting Athenian naval victory: "[The Athenians] came to believe that, if they did their part resolutely, final victory was still possible."[6]

Their belief was wrong. Their city would never again be as important in Greek politics as it had been for more than a century.

Chronology

All dates BCE

484   Possible birth date, in Halicarnassus, of Herodotus

  *   Participates in revolt against Lygdamis, the ruler of Halicarnassus

  *   Exiled to island of Samos

  *   Returns to Halicarnassus as part of another revolt against Lygdamis; this one is successful

  *   Begins series of travels

  *   Visits Egypt

  *   Begins giving public performances

  *   Lives in Athens for a while

445   May have received payment from Athens to settle there

443   May have settled in Athenian colony of Thurii

  *   Travels through Greece; begins writing *Histories*

  *   Publishes *Histories*

424   Possible date of death, probably in Thurii

* *While the relative order of these events has been determined, their exact dates are not known.*

BIOGRAPHY FROM
ANCIENT CIVILIZATIONS
LEGENDS, FOLKLORE, AND STORIES OF ANCIENT WORLDS

Timeline in History

All dates BCE

c. 850	Homer records *The Iliad* and *The Odyssey.*
546	Persians conquer Greek cities in Asia Minor.
522	Darius becomes king of Persia.
510	The tyrant Hippias is expelled from Athens.
507	Cleisthenes leads movement toward democracy in Athens.
499	Ionian Greek colonies revolt against Persian rule.
494	Persians put down rebellion of Ionian Greeks.
490	Athenians defeat Persians at the Battle of Marathon.
486	Darius dies; his son Xerxes I succeeds him.
480	Greeks win Battle of Salamis.
479	Greeks win Battle of Plataea, ending threat of Persian invasion.
470	Greek philosopher Socrates is born.
465	Xerxes is assassinated.
c. 460	Greek historian Thucydides is born.
431	Peloponnesian War begins.
413	Athens suffers disastrous defeat at Syracuse, Sicily.
404	Peloponnesian War ends with Spartan victory.
c. 400	Thucydides dies.
399	Socrates is executed after being convicted of impiety and corrupting the minds of the young.
356	Alexander the Great is born.
336	Alexander becomes king of Macedonia after the death of his father, Philip.
323	Alexander dies after conquering an empire of more than two million square miles.

Chapter Notes

Chapter 1
An Historic First, and the First History

1. Herodotus, *The Histories,* translated by Aubrey de Sélincourt (New York: Penguin Books, 1996), pp. 358–359.

Chapter 3
The World According to Herodotus

1. Herodotus, *The Histories,* translated by Aubrey de Sélincourt (New York: Penguin Books, 1996), p. 497.

2. Ibid., p. 3.

3. John Marincola, *Greek Historians* (London: Oxford University Press, 2001), p. 53.

4. J.A.S. Evans, *Herodotus* (Boston: Twayne Publishers, 1982), p. 20.

5. Herodotus, p. 98.

6. Ibid.

7. Ibid., pp. 194–195.

8. Ibid., p. 195.

Chapter 4
Jolting the Persian Juggernaut

1. Herodotus, *The Histories,* translated by Aubrey de Sélincourt (New York: Penguin Books, 1996), p. 362.

2. Ibid., p. 372.

3. Ibid., p. 413.

4. Ibid., p. 415.

5. Ibid., p. 416.

6. Barry Strauss, *The Battle of Salamis: The Naval Encounter That Saved Greece—and Western Civilization* (New York: Simon and Schuster, 2004), p. 159.

7. Herodotus, pp. 402–403.

8. Ibid., p. 477.

9. Ibid., p. 482.

10. Ibid.

Chapter 5
After Herodotus

1. Thucydides, *History of the Peloponnesian War,* translated by Rex Warner (New York: Penguin Books, 1972), p. 48.

2. J.A.S. Evans, *Herodotus* (Boston: Twayne Publishers, 1982), pp. 165–166.

3. Barry Strauss, *The Battle of Salamis: The Naval Encounter That Saved Greece—and Western Civilization* (New York: Simon and Schuster, 2004), p. 6.

4. Herodotus, *The Histories,* translated by Aubrey de Sélincourt (New York: Penguin Books, 1996), p. 307.

5. Ibid., p. 37.

6. Thucydides, p. 604.

Further Reading

For Young Adults

Freeman, Charles. *The Ancient Greeks.* New York: Oxford University Press, 1994.

Gaines, Ann. *Herodotus and the Explorers of the Classical Age.* Philadelphia: Chelsea House, 1994.

Nardo, Don. *The Battle of Marathon.* San Diego: Lucent Books, 1996.

Pearson, Anne. *Eyewitness: Ancient Greece.* New York: DK Publishing, 2004.

Rees, Rosemary. *The Ancient Greeks.* Crystal Lake, Illinois: Heinemann Library, 1997.

Whiting, Jim. *The Life and Times of Pericles.* Hockessin, Delaware: Mitchell Lane Publishers, 2005.

Zeinert, Karen. *The Persian Empire.* New York: Benchmark Books, 1997.

Works Consulted

Evans, J.A.S. *Herodotus.* Boston: Twayne Publishers, 1982.

———. *Herodotus, Explorer of the Past.* Princeton, New Jersey: Princeton University Press, 1991.

Gould, John. *Herodotus.* London: Weidenfeld and Nicolson, 1989.

Hart, John. *Herodotus and Greek History.* New York: St. Martin's Press, 1982.

Herodotus. *The Histories.* Translated by Aubrey de Sélincourt. New York: Penguin Books, 1996.

Marincola, John. *Greek Historians.* London: Oxford University Press, 2001.

Strauss, Barry. *The Battle of Salamis: The Naval Encounter That Saved Greece— and Western Civilization.* New York: Simon and Schuster, 2004.

Thucydides. *History of the Peloponnesian War.* Translated by Rex Warner. New York: Penguin Books, 1972.

On the Internet

Hellenic Ministry of Culture: "Cultural Map of Hellas."
http://www.culture.gr/2/21/maps/ hellas.html

Herodotus Website.
http://www.herodotuswebsite.co.uk

The Hoplite Experience.
http://www.holycross.edu/ departments/classics/dawhite/

Knox, E.L. Skip. "Ancient History: The Peloponnesian War."
http://history.boisestate.edu/ westciv/peloponn/

Roach, John. "Delphic Oracle's Lips May Have Been Loosened by Gas Vapors." *National Geographic News*, August 14, 2001.
http://news.nationalgeographic.com/ news/2001/08/ 0814_delphioracle.html

University of Pennsylvania Museum of Archaeology and Anthropology: "The Ancient Greek World."
http://www.museum.upenn.edu/ Greek_World/Index.html

Glossary

archaeology	(ar-kee-AH-luh-jee)—the scientific study of the lives and habits of ancient civilizations.
caches	(KASH-ez)—piles of stored goods and equipment.
cadence	(KAY-dents)—the regular rhythm of an activity.
conduit	(KAHN-doo-it)—a passage through which something (such as air or water) is carried or funneled.
exiled	(EK-ziled)—forced to leave one's homeland.
hallucinogenic	(huh-LOO-suh-nuh-JEN-ik)—producing vivid, colorful visions.
peers	people of a similar social or economic status.
poleis	(POE-lase)—plural of *polis*.
polis	(POE-liss)—a Greek city-state, consisting of a central town or city and the surrounding countryside.
savvy	(SAA-vee)—clever, wise; having practical know-how.
shirk	shrug off; avoid.
tribute	(TRIH-byoot)—payment from one nation to another in recognition of the second nation's superiority.
truce	(TROOS)—an agreement to stop fighting.
usurpers	(yoo-SUR-purs)—people who take over a government by force.

Index

Aminias   35

Anytus   15

Artemisia   35–36

Cambyses   23, 24

Cicero   39

Croesus   17, 22–23

Cyrus   17, 22–23

Darius   24, 27, 28

Datis   27

Delian League   20

Delphic Oracle   23, 25, 30–31

Dryo (mother)   13

Eurybiades   31, 32

Herodotus

    birth of   10, 13

    death of   16

    education of   13–14

    purpose of *Histories*   19–20, 21

    settles in Thurii   15

    reputation of   39, 41, 42

    travels of   12, 13, 14–15, 16, 19

    Hippias   27

Homer   17

hoplites   8, 11

Ionian Greeks   13, 17, 24, 28

Lygdamis   14, 35

Lyxes (father)   13

Marathon, Battle of   7–10, 11, 27–28

Mardonius   36

Olympic Games   10

Panyassis (uncle)   13, 14

Parthenon   9, 20, 21

Peloponnesian War   16, 39, 40, 42

Pericles   14, 15, 42

Persian War   7–10, 19, 20–24, 27–36

Pheidippides   9–10, 27

Plataea, Battle of   17, 36

Salamis, Battle of   6, 26, 29–36

Sinnicus   32–33

Themistocles   30–34

Thermopylae, Battle of   29, 31

Thucydides   20, 39–40, 42

Thurii   15, 16

Trojan War   22

Xerxes   28, 29, 30, 32–36